Faux Calligraphy For Beginners

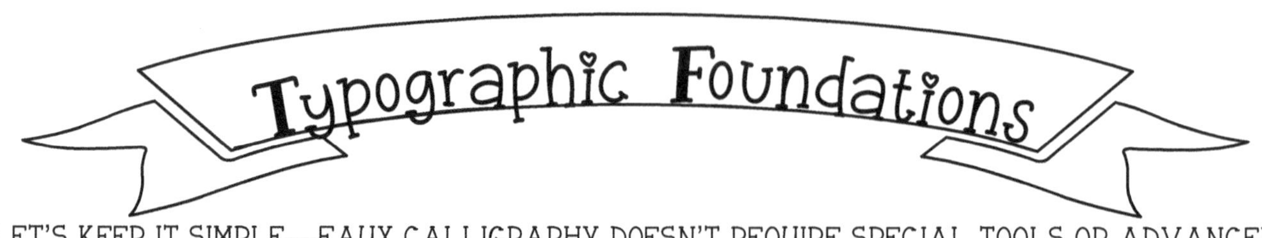

LET'S KEEP IT SIMPLE—FAUX CALLIGRAPHY DOESN'T REQUIRE SPECIAL TOOLS OR ADVANCED TECHNIQUES. INSTEAD, IT'S ABOUT CREATING THE LOOK OF TRADITIONAL CALLIGRAPHY USING ANY STANDARD PEN OR PENCIL. THE SECRET? CAREFULLY ADDING WEIGHT TO YOUR DOWNSTROKES WHILE KEEPING UPSTROKES THIN.

BUT BEFORE YOU START, FOCUS ON THE ESSENTIALS: GOOD POSTURE, A STEADY GRIP, AND THE RIGHT PAPER. THESE FOUNDATIONS WILL HELP YOU CRAFT SMOOTH, BALANCED LETTERS AND GIVE YOUR WRITING THAT ELEGANT, HAND-LETTERED STYLE. MASTERING THESE BASICS WILL ALLOW YOUR CREATIVITY TO FLOW, TURNING SIMPLE STROKES INTO BEAUTIFULLY LETTERED WORDS.

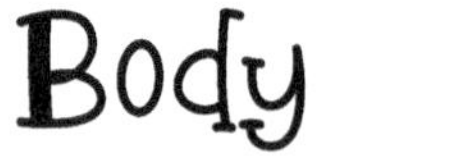

THINK POSTURE DOESN'T MATTER? THINK AGAIN! IN FAUX CALLIGRAPHY, PRECISION AND CONTROL ARE EVERYTHING. SIT COMFORTABLY—MAYBE AT A DESK WHERE YOUR FEET REST FLAT ON THE GROUND AND YOUR ARM HAS THE SPACE TO MOVE FREELY. THE MAGIC HAPPENS WHEN YOU CAREFULLY SHAPE EACH LETTER, NOT JUST RELY ON FLUID STROKES.

UNLIKE TRADITIONAL CALLIGRAPHY, FAUX CALLIGRAPHY REQUIRES SKETCHING LETTERFORMS RATHER THAN WRITING IN ONE MOTION. FOCUS ON STEADY MOVEMENTS, ADDING THICKNESS TO DOWNSTROKES WHILE KEEPING UPSTROKES THIN. IMAGINE YOU'RE CRAFTING EACH LETTER WITH INTENTION—STRUCTURED, BALANCED, AND FULL OF STYLE.

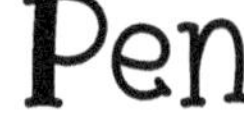

YOUR PEN IS YOUR CREATIVE TOOL, AND IN FAUX CALLIGRAPHY, YOU DON'T NEED ANYTHING FANCY. WHETHER IT'S A PENCIL, BALLPOINT, OR FINELINER, THE BEST TOOL IS SIMPLY THE ONE YOU HAVE ON HAND. HOLD IT COMFORTABLY, WITH A STEADY BUT RELAXED GRIP.

DON'T STRESS OVER PERFECTION—YOUR FIRST LETTERS MAY LOOK UNEVEN, AND THAT'S OKAY. THE KEY IS TO SKETCH YOUR STROKES CAREFULLY, THEN GO BACK AND ADD THICKNESS TO THE DOWNSTROKES. FAUX CALLIGRAPHY IS ALL ABOUT EXPERIMENTING, REFINING, AND SLOWLY DEVELOPING YOUR OWN UNIQUE LETTERING STYLE.

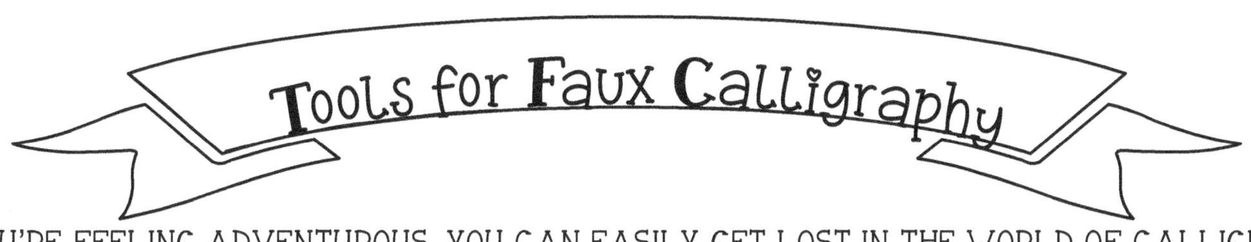

IF YOU'RE FEELING ADVENTUROUS, YOU CAN EASILY GET LOST IN THE WORLD OF CALLIGRAPHY SUPPLIES—AND YES, IT'S TEMPTING TO TRY THEM ALL! IF THAT'S YOUR STYLE, GO FOR IT! BUT WITH FAUX CALLIGRAPHY, SIMPLICITY IS KEY. YOU DON'T NEED EXPENSIVE TOOLS—JUST A BASIC PEN OR PENCIL. IF YOU'RE CURIOUS, HERE'S A BREAKDOWN OF SOME USEFUL OPTIONS:

★ PENCILS

THE BEST PLACE TO START—SIMPLE, RELIABLE, AND PERFECT FOR SKETCHING LETTERFORMS BEFORE INKING.

★ PENS

NOT SURE WHERE TO BEGIN? A BALLPOINT, GEL PEN, OR FINELINER WORKS GREAT. THEY ALLOW FOR SMOOTH, PRECISE STROKES WHEN BUILDING YOUR FAUX CALLIGRAPHY STYLE.

★ MARKERS

IF YOU WANT A BOLDER LOOK, TRY USING A MARKER. THE THICKER LINES CAN MAKE YOUR DOWNSTROKES STAND OUT EVEN MORE.

★ ERASERS

A MUST-HAVE WHEN SKETCHING YOUR LETTERS WITH A PENCIL. HELPS REFINE YOUR SHAPES BEFORE COMMITTING TO INK.

★ RULER

USEFUL FOR CREATING GUIDELINES TO MAINTAIN CONSISTENCY IN YOUR LETTERING.

FAUX CALLIGRAPHY IS ALL ABOUT ACCESSIBILITY—YOU CAN CREATE BEAUTIFUL, HAND-LETTERED DESIGNS WITH WHATEVER TOOLS YOU ALREADY HAVE. NO BRUSH PENS REQUIRED!

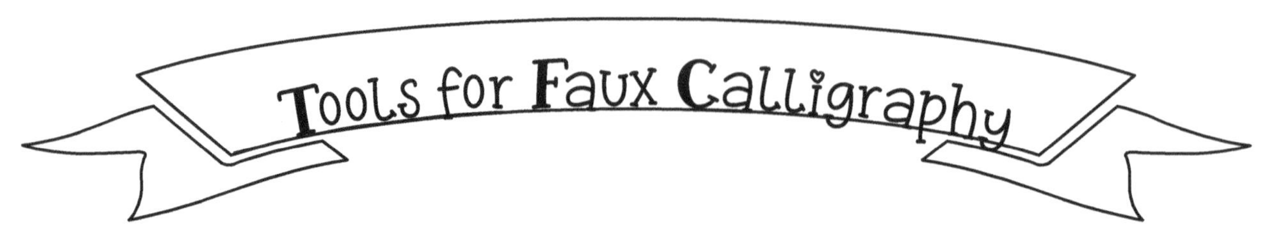

★ CHALK

CHALK LETTERING IS A FUN WAY TO APPLY FAUX CALLIGRAPHY TECHNIQUES. CHALK MARKERS MAKE IT EASY TO CREATE STUNNING CHALKBOARD DESIGNS, PERFECT FOR CAFE MENUS, EVENT SIGNAGE, OR CREATIVE PROJECTS.

★ PAPER

THIS BOOK PROVIDES PLENTY OF SPACE FOR PRACTICE, BUT CHOOSING THE RIGHT PAPER CAN IMPROVE YOUR RESULTS. OPT FOR SMOOTH, HEAVYWEIGHT PAPER LIKE CARDSTOCK FOR CRISP, CLEAN STROKES. AVOID THIN PRINTER PAPER, WHICH CAN CAUSE INK TO FEATHER OR SMUDGE.

★ FINELINER PENS

A FINE-TIP PEN OR GEL PEN IS A MUST-HAVE FOR FAUX CALLIGRAPHY. THESE PENS MAKE IT EASY TO OUTLINE YOUR LETTERS AND THICKEN THE DOWNSTROKES WITHOUT NEEDING A BRUSH PEN.

★ MARKERS

IF YOU PREFER A BOLDER LOOK, MARKERS WORK WELL FOR FAUX CALLIGRAPHY. USE THEM TO CREATE STRIKING DOWNSTROKES AND ADD EXTRA DEPTH TO YOUR LETTERING.

THE BEST PART ABOUT FAUX CALLIGRAPHY IS THAT YOU DON'T NEED SPECIAL TOOLS—JUST A SIMPLE PEN AND SOME CREATIVITY TO ACHIEVE ELEGANT, HAND-LETTERED DESIGNS.

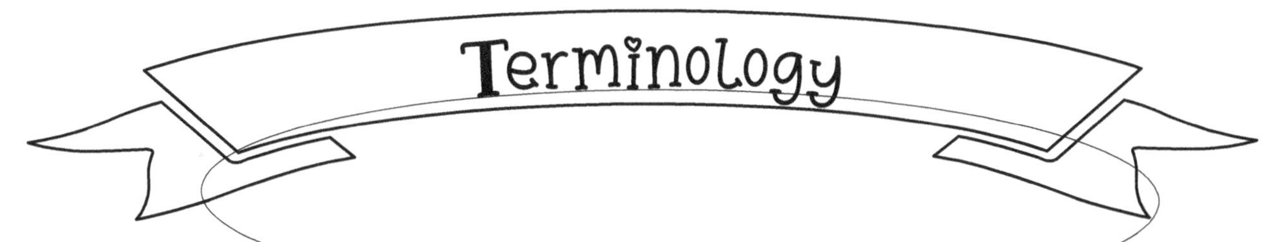

BEFORE YOU START CREATING BEAUTIFUL LETTERS, IT'S IMPORTANT TO UNDERSTAND SOME KEY TERMS. THINK OF IT AS LEARNING THE FOUNDATION BEFORE BUILDING WORDS—SO DON'T SKIP THIS STEP. MASTERING THESE BASICS WILL MAKE YOUR FAUX CALLIGRAPHY JOURNEY MUCH EASIER AND MORE ENJOYABLE.

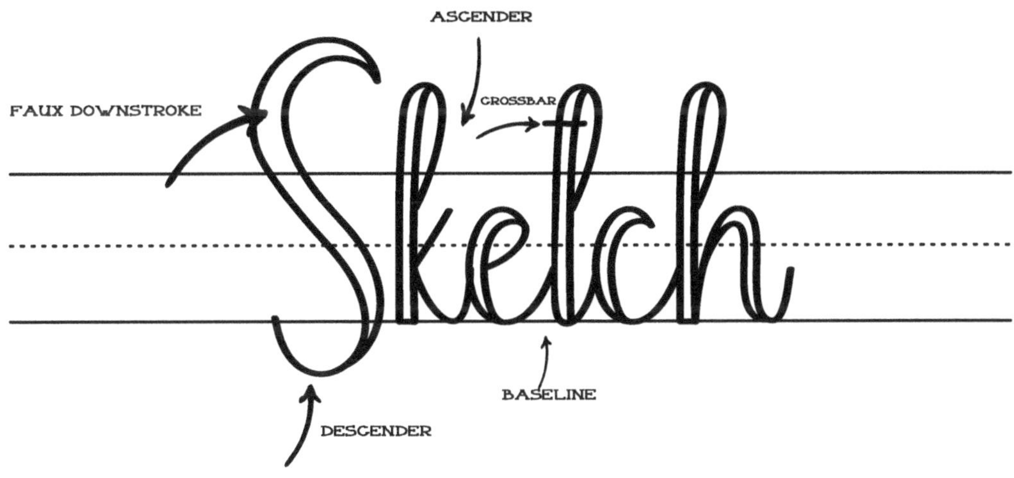

★ FAUX DOWNSTROKE

IN FAUX CALLIGRAPHY, DOWNSTROKES ARE MANUALLY THICKENED TO CREATE THE ILLUSION OF TRADITIONAL CALLIGRAPHY. THESE STROKES ADD DEPTH AND CONTRAST WITHOUT USING A BRUSH PEN.

★ ASCENDER

THE PART OF A LETTER THAT RISES ABOVE THE MEDIAN LINE, AS SEEN IN THE TALL STROKES OF "K" AND "T." ASCENDERS HELP DEFINE THE HEIGHT AND STRUCTURE OF THE WORD.

★ DESCENDER

THE PORTION OF A LETTER THAT EXTENDS BELOW THE BASELINE, LIKE THE CURVED TAIL OF THE "S" IN "SKETCH." DESCENDERS ADD BALANCE AND VISUAL INTEREST.

★ CROSSBAR

A HORIZONTAL STROKE THAT CONNECTS PARTS OF A LETTER, SUCH AS THE CROSS ON THE "T." THIS ELEMENT HELPS MAINTAIN CONSISTENCY AND READABILITY IN FAUX CALLIGRAPHY.

★ BASELINE

THE LINE ON WHICH MOST LETTERS SIT, ENSURING ALIGNMENT AND UNIFORMITY IN WRITING. IT SERVES AS THE FOUNDATION FOR BALANCED AND WELL-STRUCTURED LETTERS.

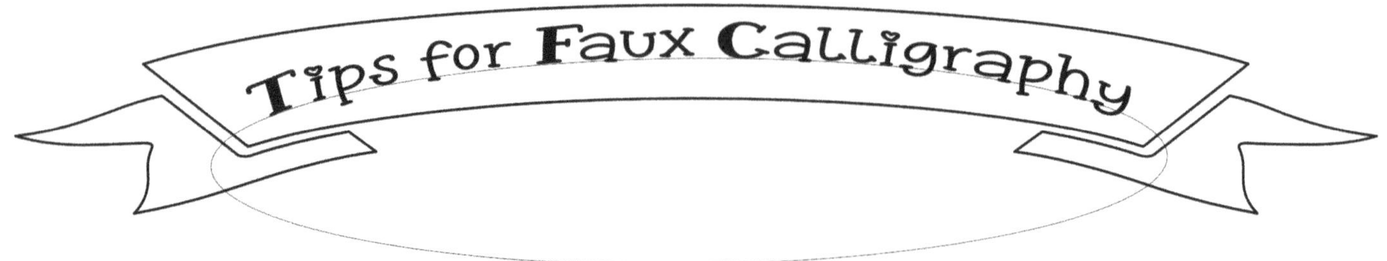

ONE

SLOW AND STEADY WINS THE RACE! THINK OF EACH LETTER AS A SMALL PIECE OF ART—CAREFULLY DRAWN RATHER THAN QUICKLY WRITTEN LIKE REGULAR HANDWRITING.

TWO

START WITH A PENCIL—IT'S YOUR BEST TOOL FOR REFINING SHAPES. SKETCH, ERASE, AND ADJUST YOUR LETTERS UNTIL THEY LOOK JUST RIGHT. MISTAKES ARE PART OF THE LEARNING PROCESS!

THREE

LIFT YOUR PEN AFTER EACH STROKE. UNLIKE CURSIVE WRITING, WHERE LETTERS FLOW TOGETHER, FAUX CALLIGRAPHY IS BUILT IN SEPARATE STROKES, ALLOWING FOR MORE PRECISION AND CONTROL.

FOUR

THE KEY TO FAUX CALLIGRAPHY IS THICKENING ONLY THE DOWNWARD STROKES. MANUALLY ADD WEIGHT TO THESE LINES TO CREATE THE SIGNATURE CONTRAST OF TRADITIONAL CALLIGRAPHY.

FIVE

UPWARD STROKES SHOULD REMAIN THIN. INSTEAD OF USING PRESSURE TO VARY THICKNESS, CAREFULLY OUTLINE YOUR DOWNSTROKES AND LEAVE UPSTROKES UNTOUCHED.

SIX

PRACTICE, PRACTICE, PRACTICE! FIRST, MASTER INDIVIDUAL LETTER SHAPES. THEN, CONNECT THEM INTO WORDS. ONCE YOU GAIN CONFIDENCE, EXPERIMENT WITH LAYOUTS AND DECORATIVE ELEMENTS TO MAKE YOUR LETTERING TRULY UNIQUE.

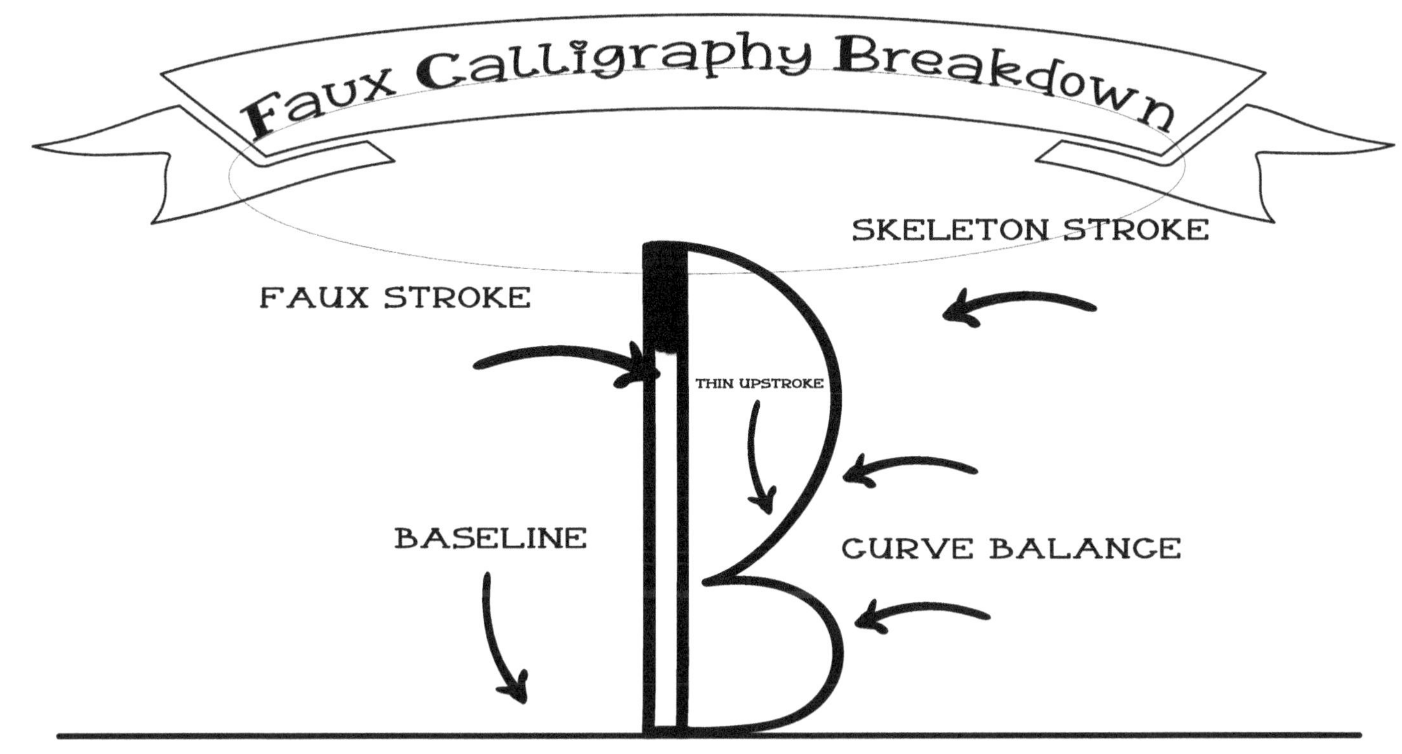

SKELETON STROKE — THE BASE STRUCTURE OF THE LETTER "B," DRAWN WITH A SINGLE, THIN LINE BEFORE ADDING WEIGHT TO THE DOWNSTROKES. THIS ACTS AS A GUIDE FOR THE FINAL FAUX CALLIGRAPHY EFFECT.

FAUX DOWNSTROKE — THE THICKER SECTIONS OF THE LETTER, MANUALLY ADDED TO MIMIC BRUSH CALLIGRAPHY. IN THE LETTER "B," THE LEFT VERTICAL STROKE IS THICKENED, ALONG WITH THE INNER CURVES ON THE RIGHT SIDE WHERE DOWNWARD MOTION WOULD NATURALLY OCCUR.

THIN UPSTROKE — THE AREAS WHERE THE STROKE MOVES UPWARD REMAIN THIN, CREATING CONTRAST. IN "B," THIS APPLIES TO THE TOP RIGHT CURVE LEADING INTO THE DOWNSTROKE.

BASELINE — THE HORIZONTAL GUIDELINE ON WHICH THE LETTER RESTS, ENSURING CONSISTENT ALIGNMENT WITH OTHER LETTERS.

CURVE BALANCE — THE ROUNDED PORTIONS OF THE "B" SHOULD MAINTAIN EVEN PROPORTIONS, WITH DOWNSTROKES SLIGHTLY HEAVIER THAN UPSTROKES TO CREATE A NATURAL CALLIGRAPHY EFFECT.

Basic strokes
Introduction

ALSO CALLED "FAUX CALLIGRAPHY," THIS TECHNIQUE IS A GREAT STARTING POINT FOR LEARNING HAND LETTERING. WHILE THICK, BOLD STROKES ARE A SIGNATURE OF TRADITIONAL CALLIGRAPHY, FAUX CALLIGRAPHY LETS YOU ACHIEVE THE SAME ELEGANT LOOK WITH ANY BASIC PEN OR PENCIL.

INSTEAD OF ADJUSTING PRESSURE LIKE IN BRUSH LETTERING, YOU START WITH A SIMPLE MONOLINE STRUCTURE AND MANUALLY THICKEN THE DOWNSTROKES TO CREATE CONTRAST. NO SPECIAL TOOLS REQUIRED—JUST A PENCIL OR A FINE-TIP PEN (THE SMALLER, THE BETTER) TO SKETCH, REFINE, AND BRING YOUR LETTERS TO LIFE WITH EASE!

First Step:
Draw the basic letter with thin, even strokes.

Finish:
Thicken the downstrokes to create the faux calligraphy effect.

To make the most of your faux calligraphy practice, it's essential to understand how strokes work. Unlike traditional calligraphy, where pressure variation creates thick and thin lines, faux calligraphy requires you to manually add weight to your downstrokes while keeping your upstrokes thin and delicate.

Why Faux Calligraphy Works for Beginners

No special tools needed – you can achieve a calligraphy-style look with any basic pen, pencil, or marker.

More control – because you aren't relying on pressure, you have more precision over your letterforms.

Easy to learn – faux calligraphy follows simple rules: draw your letters as you normally would, then go back and thicken only the downward strokes.

Great for any surface – unlike brush pens, which require smooth, high-quality paper, faux calligraphy can be done on notebooks, planners, or even chalkboards.

Tips for Practicing Faux Calligraphy

Keep your upstrokes light – thin, even strokes will enhance the contrast between thick and thin sections.

Be consistent – try to keep your downstroke thickness uniform throughout a word.

Use guidelines – keeping your letters aligned helps improve readability and spacing.

Experiment with styles – once you're comfortable, try different letter variations and flourishes.

With time and practice, you'll master faux calligraphy and be able to create elegant, hand-lettered designs with ease! Now, grab your pen and start practicing!

High Strokes

- MASTERING HIGH STROKES IS ESSENTIAL FOR ACHIEVING CONSISTENT LETTER HEIGHT AND UNIFORMITY IN FAUX CALLIGRAPHY. THESE STROKES SERVE AS THE FOUNDATION FOR MANY UPPERCASE AND LOWERCASE LETTERS, PARTICULARLY THOSE WITH TALL ASCENDERS LIKE L, H, B, AND K.

STEP 1: DRAW THE BASE STROKE

- START FROM THE BASELINE AND MOVE UPWARD IN A SMOOTH, CONTROLLED MOTION. UNLIKE BRUSH CALLIGRAPHY, WHERE PRESSURE IS ADJUSTED, FAUX CALLIGRAPHY REQUIRES MAINTAINING A THIN, EVEN STROKE THROUGHOUT THE ENTIRE MOVEMENT.

STEP 2: FOCUS ON CONSISTENCY

- EACH STROKE SHOULD HAVE A UNIFORM THICKNESS—AVOID PRESSING TOO HARD OR ACCIDENTALLY VARYING THE WIDTH. IF YOUR LINES ARE WOBBLY, TRY SLOWING DOWN YOUR MOVEMENT AND KEEPING A STEADY RHYTHM.

STEP 3: APPLY THE STROKE TO LETTERS

- ONCE YOU HAVE MASTERED THE HIGH STROKE, USE IT IN LETTERS LIKE L, H, B, AND K WHILE ENSURING THE UPWARD MOTION REMAINS LIGHT AND GRACEFUL. SINCE FAUX CALLIGRAPHY RELIES ON ADDING WEIGHT ONLY TO DOWNSTROKES, HIGH STROKES WILL ALWAYS REMAIN THIN AND UNALTERED.

FINAL CHECK

- YOUR STROKES SHOULD BE EVENLY SPACED AND CONSISTENTLY SHAPED. PRACTICING HIGH STROKES WILL HELP CREATE POLISHED, ELEGANT LETTERFORMS IN YOUR FAUX CALLIGRAPHY.

Upturn

- AN UPTURN IS A FUNDAMENTAL STROKE IN FAUX CALLIGRAPHY, APPEARING IN LETTERS THAT REQUIRE GENTLE, CURVED TRANSITIONS LIKE U, N, M, AND R. IT IS AN ESSENTIAL TECHNIQUE FOR CREATING SMOOTH LETTER CONNECTIONS.

STEP 1: DRAW THE UPWARD STROKE

- START WITH A THIN, EVEN STROKE AND MOVE UPWARD IN A SLIGHT CURVE. THIS MOTION SHOULD FEEL NATURAL AND FLOW SEAMLESSLY INTO THE NEXT STROKE OF THE LETTER.

STEP 2: MAINTAIN CONSISTENCY

- THE KEY TO A WELL-FORMED UPTURN IS TO KEEP THE STROKE UNIFORM IN THICKNESS—SINCE FAUX CALLIGRAPHY DOES NOT USE PRESSURE CHANGES, THIS STROKE WILL ALWAYS REMAIN THIN.

STEP 3: PREPARE FOR THE DOWNSTROKE

- ONCE THE UPTURN IS COMPLETE, THE NEXT PART OF THE LETTER WILL TYPICALLY TRANSITION INTO A DOWNWARD STROKE. THIS IS WHERE THICKNESS WILL LATER BE ADDED, SO MAINTAINING A CLEAR DISTINCTION BETWEEN THIN AND THICK SECTIONS IS CRUCIAL.

FINAL CHECK

- YOUR UPTURNS SHOULD BE SMOOTH, EVENLY SPACED, AND PROPORTIONAL. PRACTICING THIS MOTION WILL HELP IMPROVE THE NATURAL FLOW OF YOUR FAUX CALLIGRAPHY, MAKING LETTER CONNECTIONS MORE SEAMLESS..

Downward Strokes

- DOWNWARD STROKES FORM THE STRUCTURAL BACKBONE OF MANY LETTERS IN FAUX CALLIGRAPHY. THEY ARE THE SECTIONS THAT REQUIRE MANUAL THICKENING TO CREATE THE CONTRAST BETWEEN THICK AND THIN STROKES.

STEP 1: DRAW THE INITIAL STROKE

- BEGIN AT THE TOP AND MOVE DOWNWARD WITH A SMOOTH, CONTROLLED MOTION. THE INITIAL STROKE SHOULD BE THIN AND EVEN, JUST LIKE REGULAR HANDWRITING.

STEP 2: ADD FAUX THICKNESS

- SINCE FAUX CALLIGRAPHY DOES NOT RELY ON PRESSURE-SENSITIVE TOOLS, YOU WILL MANUALLY THICKEN THE DOWNSTROKE BY DRAWING A SECOND, PARALLEL LINE ALONG ONE SIDE OF THE STROKE. THIS ADDED THICKNESS SHOULD MATCH THE NATURAL FLOW OF A BRUSH PEN STROKE—GRADUALLY WIDENING TOWARDS THE MIDDLE AND TAPERING SLIGHTLY AT THE ENDS.

STEP 3: KEEP IT CONSISTENT

- WHEN ADDING THICKNESS, MAKE SURE THAT ALL YOUR DOWNSTROKES HAVE THE SAME WIDTH THROUGHOUT A WORD. IF THE DOWNSTROKES ARE INCONSISTENT, THE LETTERING MAY LOOK UNBALANCED.

FINAL CHECK

- YOUR DOWNSTROKES SHOULD BE SMOOTH, EVENLY THICKENED, AND VISUALLY COHESIVE WITH THE REST OF YOUR LETTERING. PRACTICING THIS TECHNIQUE WILL ALLOW YOU TO CREATE THE ILLUSION OF TRADITIONAL CALLIGRAPHY USING ANY PEN OR PENCIL.

Turnaround

- THE TURNAROUND STROKE IS AN ADVANCED MOVEMENT THAT HELPS CREATE FLUID, CONNECTED LETTERS IN FAUX CALLIGRAPHY. IT APPEARS IN MANY CURSIVE-STYLE LETTERS AND FLOURISHES, HELPING MAINTAIN RHYTHM IN WRITING.

STEP 1: SKETCH THE INITIAL UPSTROKE

- BEGIN WITH A THIN, STEADY UPSTROKE AND SMOOTHLY CURVE INTO A DOWNWARD MOTION. THIS TRANSITION SHOULD BE GRADUAL AND NATURAL, AVOIDING ANY SHARP OR JAGGED EDGES.

STEP 2: MAINTAIN A SMOOTH FLOW

- THE TRANSITION BETWEEN THE UPSTROKE AND DOWNSTROKE SHOULD FEEL SEAMLESS. IF YOUR CURVE IS TOO TIGHT OR ABRUPT, TRY SLIGHTLY EXTENDING THE MOTION TO CREATE A MORE GRACEFUL EFFECT.

STEP 3: ADD THICKNESS TO THE DOWNSTROKE

- ONCE THE BASIC STROKE IS COMPLETE, MANUALLY THICKEN THE DOWNWARD SECTION OF THE TURNAROUND, KEEPING THE TRANSITION INTO THE CURVE SOFT AND SMOOTH. THE ADDED WEIGHT SHOULD APPEAR NATURAL, JUST LIKE IN TRADITIONAL CALLIGRAPHY.

FINAL CHECK

- YOUR TURNAROUNDS SHOULD BE FLUID, EVENLY SHAPED, AND WELL-SPACED. PRACTICING THIS MOVEMENT WILL IMPROVE YOUR ABILITY TO CREATE DYNAMIC AND STYLISH FAUX CALLIGRAPHY COMPOSITIONS.

Ascending Loop

- MASTERING THE ASCENDING LOOP IS ESSENTIAL FOR DEVELOPING FLUID, CONTROLLED STROKES IN FAUX CALLIGRAPHY. THIS SHAPE APPEARS FREQUENTLY IN LETTERS LIKE L, H, B, AND K.

STEP 1: SKETCH THE BASE SHAPE

- BEGIN WITH A THIN, EVEN STROKE, MOVING UPWARD IN A GENTLE CURVE. KEEP YOUR MOVEMENT SLOW AND STEADY—RUSHING CAN CAUSE UNEVEN LOOPS. THE GOAL IS TO CREATE A SMOOTH, OPEN SHAPE WITH A BALANCED PROPORTION BETWEEN HEIGHT AND WIDTH.

STEP 2: ADJUST THE LOOP

- MAKE SURE THE CURVE AT THE TOP OF THE LOOP ISN'T TOO SHARP OR TOO NARROW. A WELL-FORMED LOOP SHOULD FEEL GRACEFUL AND AIRY, RATHER THAN CRAMPED OR TIGHT.

STEP 3: ADD FAUX DOWNSTROKES

- IN FAUX CALLIGRAPHY, WE DON'T USE PRESSURE TO THICKEN STROKES. INSTEAD, MANUALLY THICKEN THE DOWNWARD PART OF THE LOOP BY DRAWING A SECOND, PARALLEL LINE ALONG THE INNER EDGE OF THE CURVE. FILL IN THE SPACE TO CREATE THE ILLUSION OF A NATURAL BRUSH PEN STROKE.

FINAL CHECK

- YOUR LOOP SHOULD NOW HAVE A LIGHT UPSTROKE AND A BOLD DOWNSTROKE, MIMICKING THE CONTRAST OF TRADITIONAL CALLIGRAPHY. KEEP PRACTICING TO ACHIEVE CONSISTENCY ACROSS ALL LOOPS.

Descending Loop

- THE DESCENDING LOOP IS THE FOUNDATION OF SMOOTH, FLOWING DESCENDERS IN FAUX CALLIGRAPHY. YOU'LL SEE THIS STROKE IN LETTERS LIKE G, J, Y, AND F.

STEP 1: OUTLINE THE SHAPE

- START AT THE MIDLINE AND GENTLY CURVE UPWARD, FORMING THE TOP OF THE LOOP. AS YOU TRANSITION DOWNWARD, KEEP THE LINE THIN AND EVEN—THIS IS JUST THE SKELETON OF YOUR LETTER.

STEP 2: MAINTAIN EVEN SPACING

- A WELL-BALANCED DESCENDING LOOP SHOULD HAVE A SMOOTH CURVE AND ENOUGH SPACE INSIDE THE LOOP TO MAINTAIN READABILITY. IF THE LOOP IS TOO TIGHT, YOUR LETTERING MAY LOOK CRAMPED.

STEP 3: ADD THICKNESS TO THE DOWNSTROKE

- ONCE THE BASE STROKE IS COMPLETE, MANUALLY THICKEN THE DESCENDING PART OF THE LOOP. FOLLOW THE CONTOUR OF THE ORIGINAL STROKE AND MAKE SURE THE ADDED WEIGHT IS EVEN FROM TOP TO BOTTOM.

FINAL CHECK

- COMPARE YOUR LOOPS TO ENSURE CONSISTENCY IN SIZE AND SHAPE. PRACTICING DESCENDING LOOPS WILL IMPROVE THE RHYTHM AND BALANCE OF YOUR FAUX CALLIGRAPHY.

Oval

- OVALS FORM THE FOUNDATION OF MANY LETTERS, INCLUDING O, A, D, G, AND Q. A WELL-FORMED OVAL CREATES BALANCE AND SYMMETRY IN YOUR WRITING.

STEP 1: DRAW THE BASIC SHAPE

- BEGIN WITH A THIN, EVEN OVAL, MAINTAINING A SMOOTH AND CONTINUOUS MOTION. THE ANGLE OF THE OVAL SHOULD MATCH THE OVERALL SLANT OF YOUR LETTERING STYLE.

STEP 2: DEFINE THE STROKE DIRECTION

- IN FAUX CALLIGRAPHY, THE LEFT SIDE OF THE OVAL REPRESENTS A DOWNWARD STROKE, WHILE THE RIGHT SIDE REPRESENTS AN UPWARD STROKE. KEEPING THIS IN MIND WILL HELP YOU DETERMINE WHERE TO ADD THICKNESS.

STEP 3: ADD THE FAUX DOWNSTROKE

- IDENTIFY THE HEAVIEST PART OF THE OVAL—THIS IS WHERE A BRUSH PEN WOULD NATURALLY APPLY MORE PRESSURE. MANUALLY THICKEN THE LEFT SIDE OF THE OVAL, MAKING SURE THE TRANSITION BETWEEN THIN AND THICK PARTS LOOKS SMOOTH AND INTENTIONAL.

FINAL CHECK

- YOUR OVAL SHOULD FEEL BALANCED AND PROPORTIONAL, WITHOUT AN OVERLY SHARP CONTRAST BETWEEN THE THICK AND THIN AREAS. THIS FUNDAMENTAL STROKE WILL HELP YOU CREATE CONSISTENT, POLISHED LETTERFORMS.

Compression of Turns

- SMOOTH, CONTROLLED TURNS ARE THE KEY TO FLUID LETTERING. THIS EXERCISE HELPS DEVELOP RHYTHM AND UNIFORMITY IN YOUR CALLIGRAPHY.

STEP 1: SKETCH THE BASE TURNS

- BEGIN WITH A SERIES OF CONNECTED UPWARD AND DOWNWARD STROKES, MOVING IN A WAVE-LIKE MOTION. KEEP THE SPACING BETWEEN EACH TURN CONSISTENT.

STEP 2: FOCUS ON FLOW

- THE TRANSITION BETWEEN AN UPSTROKE AND A DOWNSTROKE SHOULD FEEL NATURAL— AVOID MAKING THE TURNS TOO SHARP OR STIFF. EACH CURVE SHOULD BE SMOOTH AND EVENLY SPACED.

STEP 3: ADD WEIGHT TO DOWNSTROKES

- IDENTIFY THE LOWEST POINT OF EACH CURVE—THIS IS WHERE THE DOWNSTROKE NATURALLY OCCURS. MANUALLY ADD THICKNESS TO THESE SECTIONS WHILE KEEPING THE UPSTROKES THIN.

FINAL CHECK

- ENSURE THAT EACH TURN MAINTAINS A STEADY FLOW AND CONSISTENT WIDTH. PRACTICING THIS EXERCISE WILL MAKE IT EASIER TO CREATE FLUID, CONNECTED LETTERS IN FAUX CALLIGRAPHY.

Basic Calligraphy

UPPERCASE ALPHABET

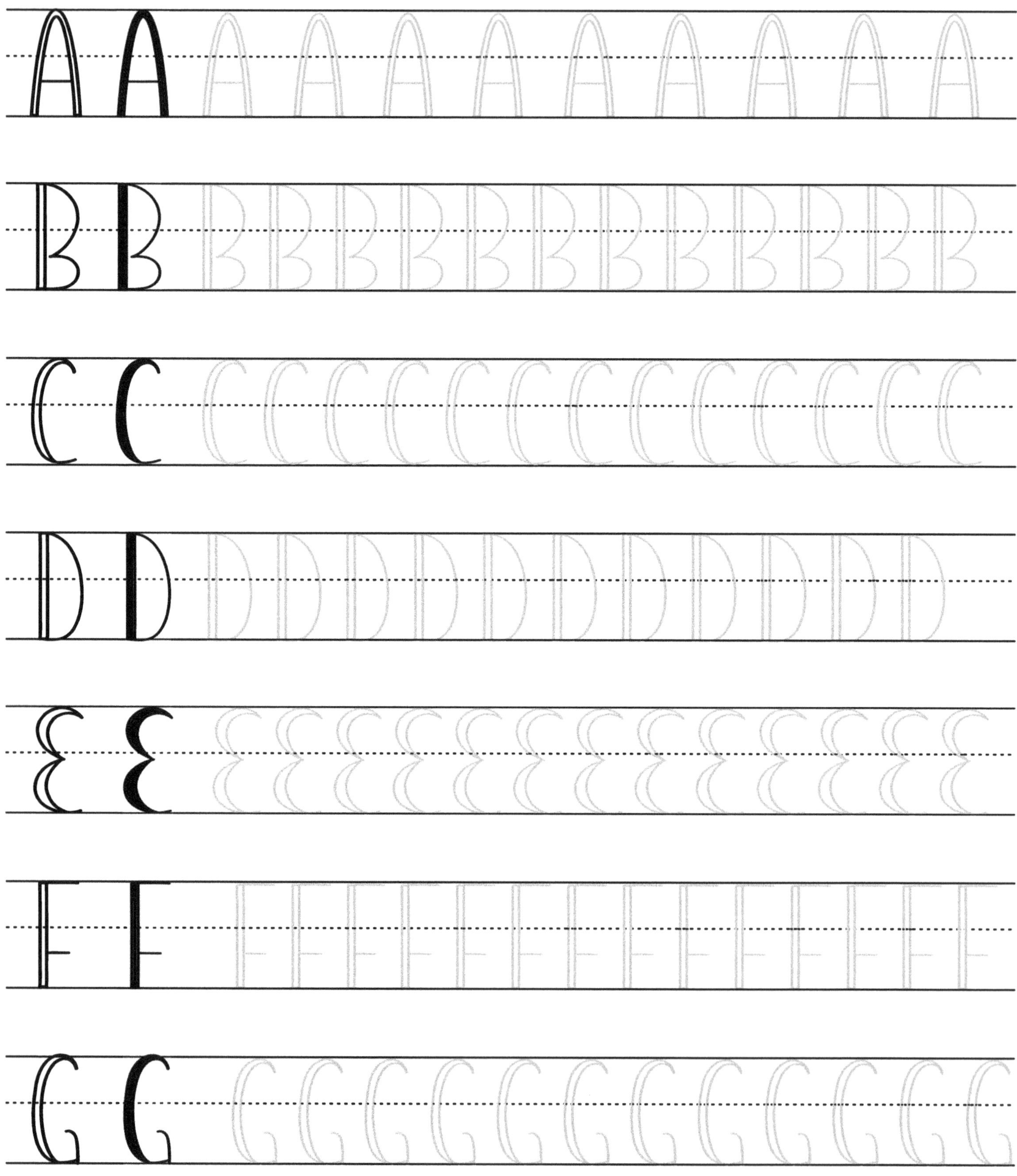

Practice Sheet

Basic Calligraphy
UPPERCASE ALPHABET

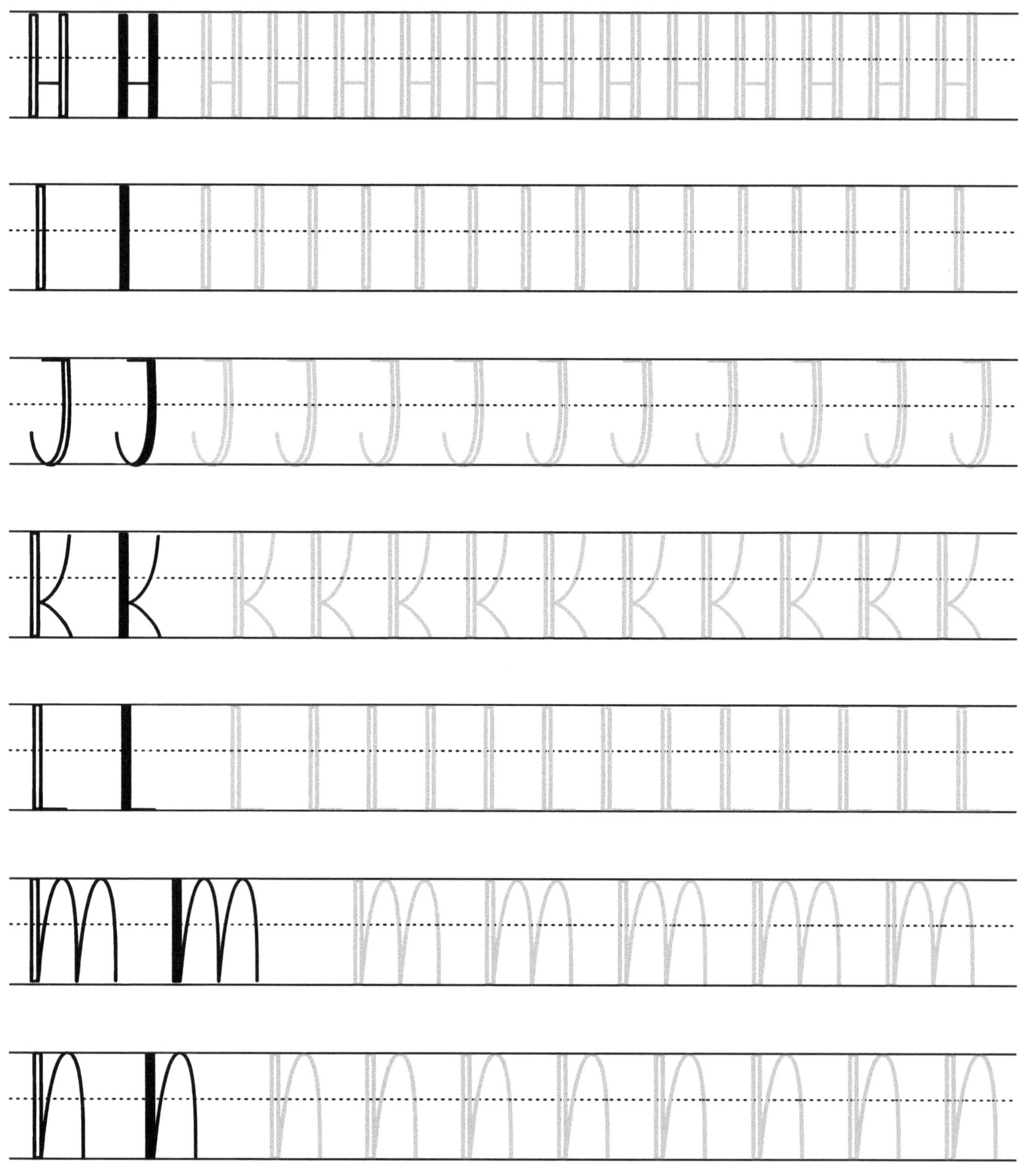

Practice Sheet

Basic Calligraphy

UPPERCASE ALPHABET

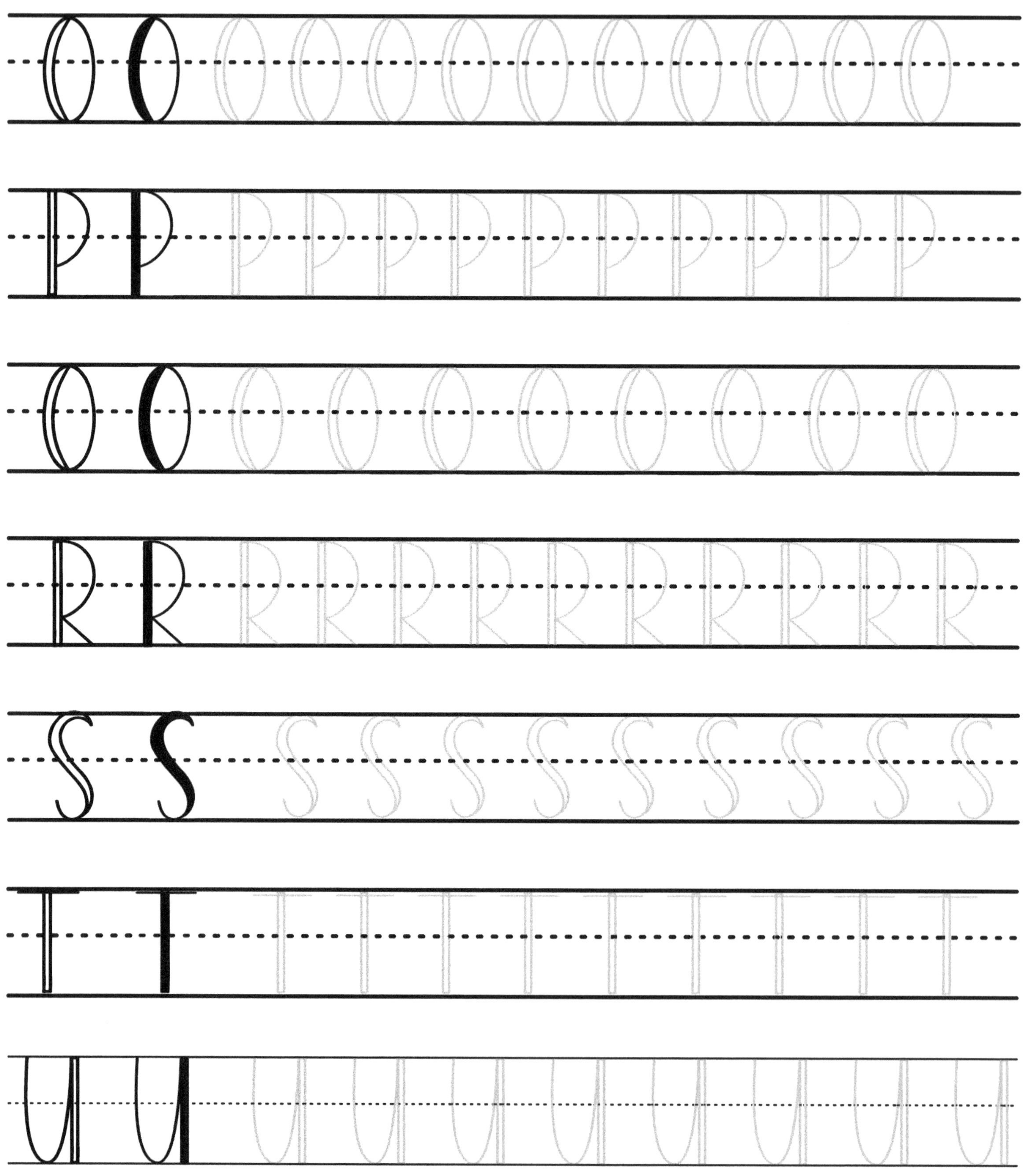

Practice Sheet

Basic Calligraphy

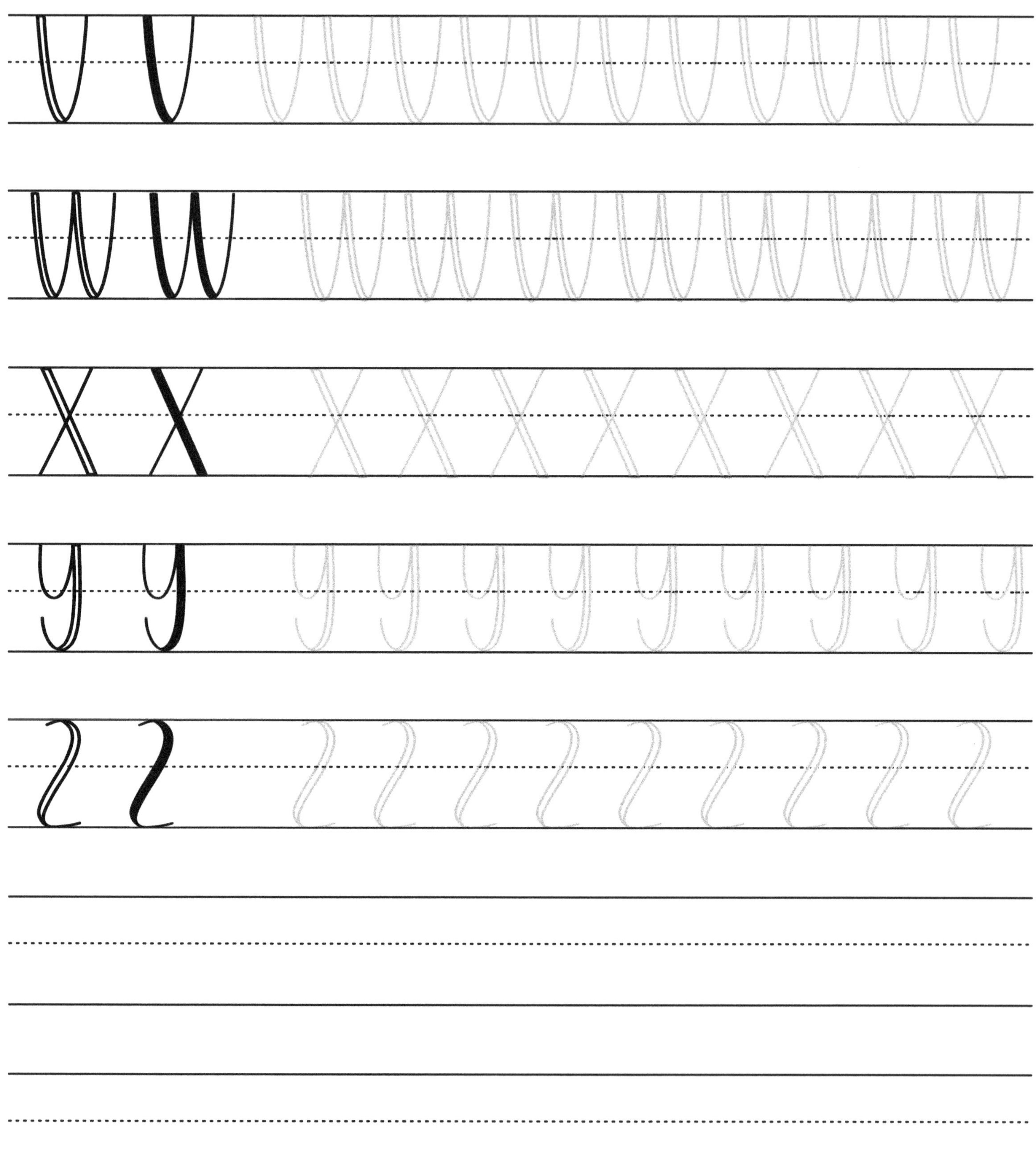

Practice Sheet

Basic Calligraphy

LOWERCASE ALPHABET

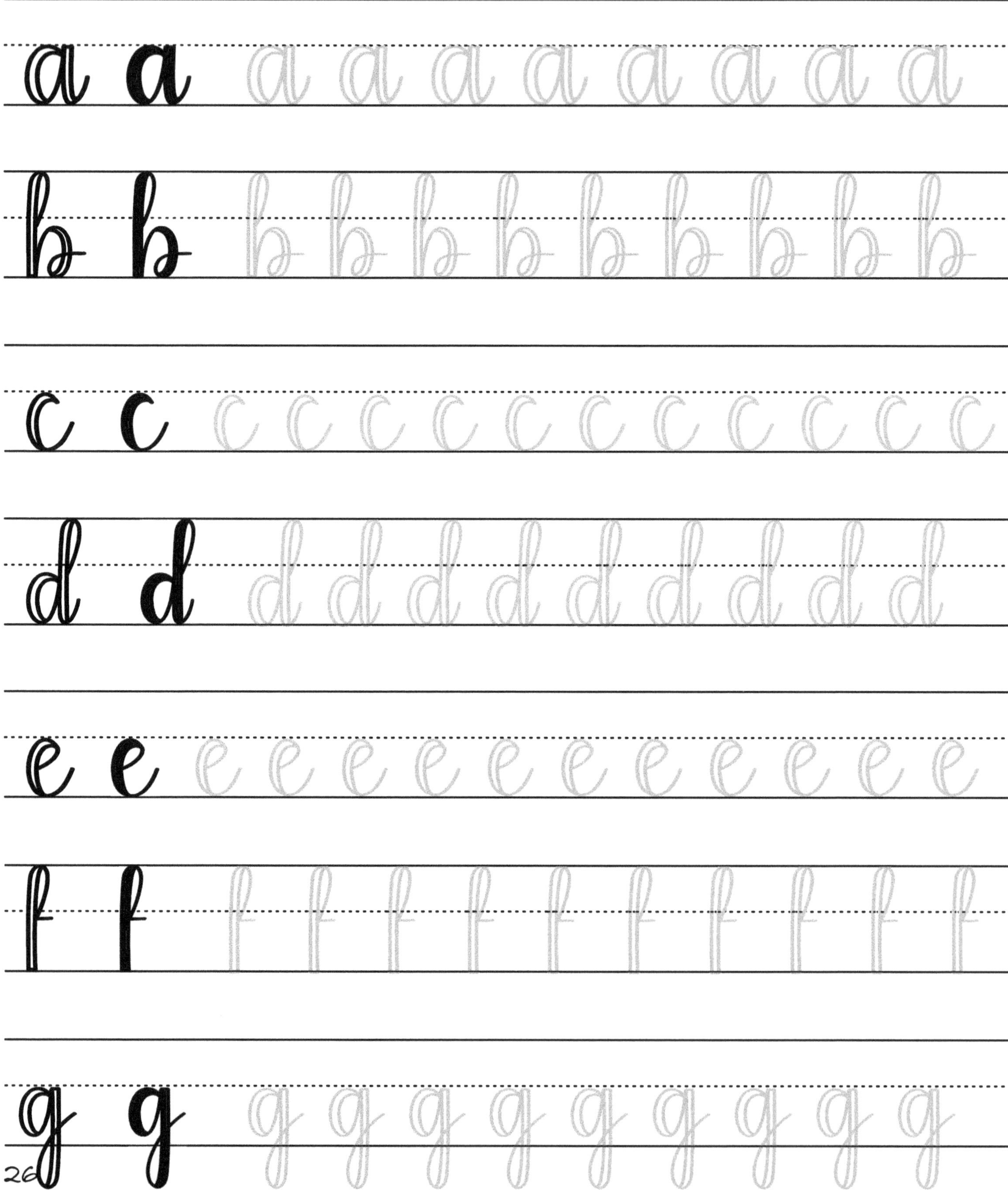

Practice Sheet

Basic Calligraphy

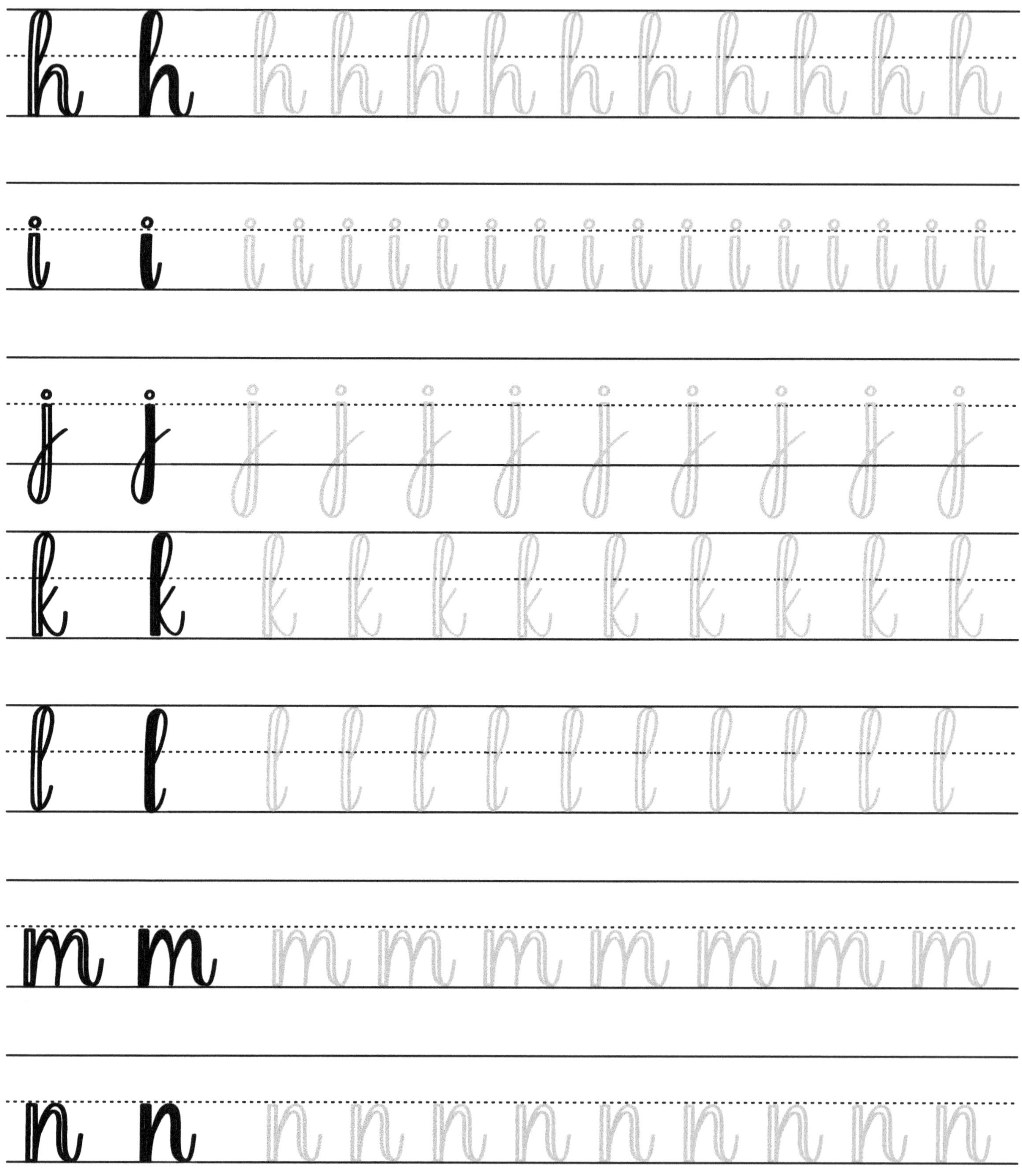

Practice Sheet

Basic Calligraphy

LOWERCASE ALPHABET

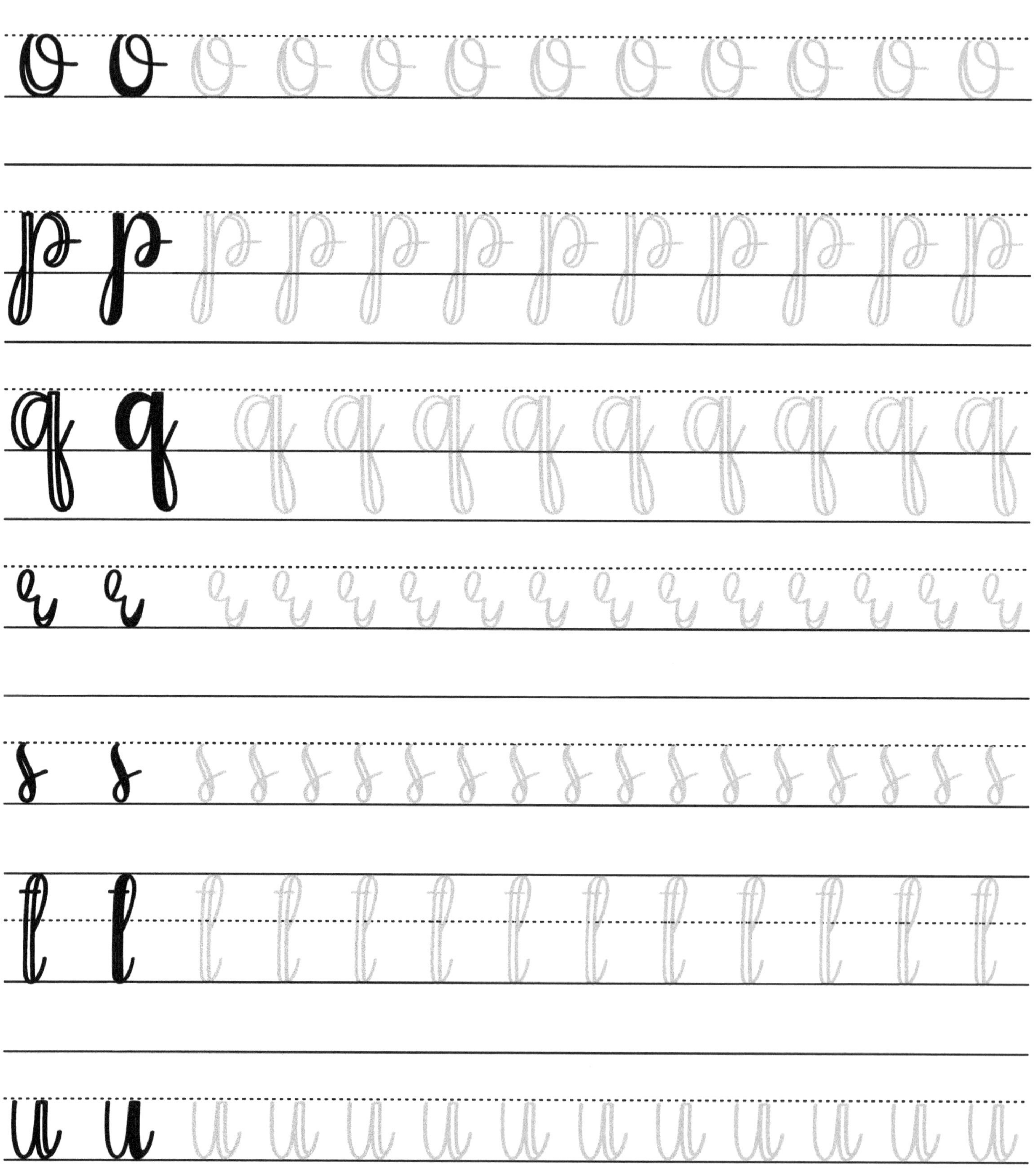

Practice Sheet

Basic Calligraphy

LOWERCASE ALPHABET

Practice Sheet

Basic Calligraphy

UPPERCASE AND LOWERCASE PRACTICE

Practice Sheet

Basic Calligraphy

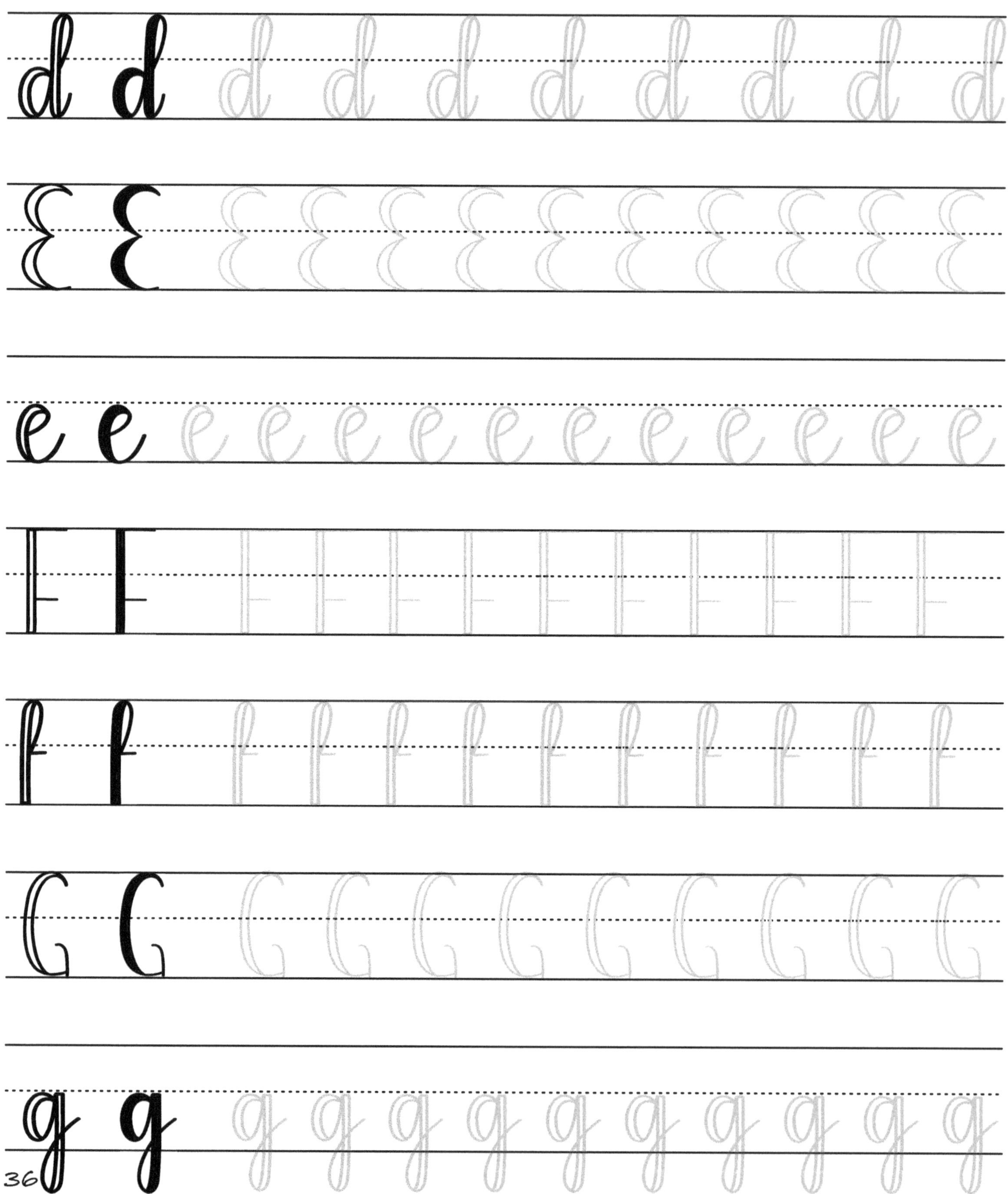

36

Practice Sheet

Basic Calligraphy

UPPERCASE AND LOWERCASE PRACTICE

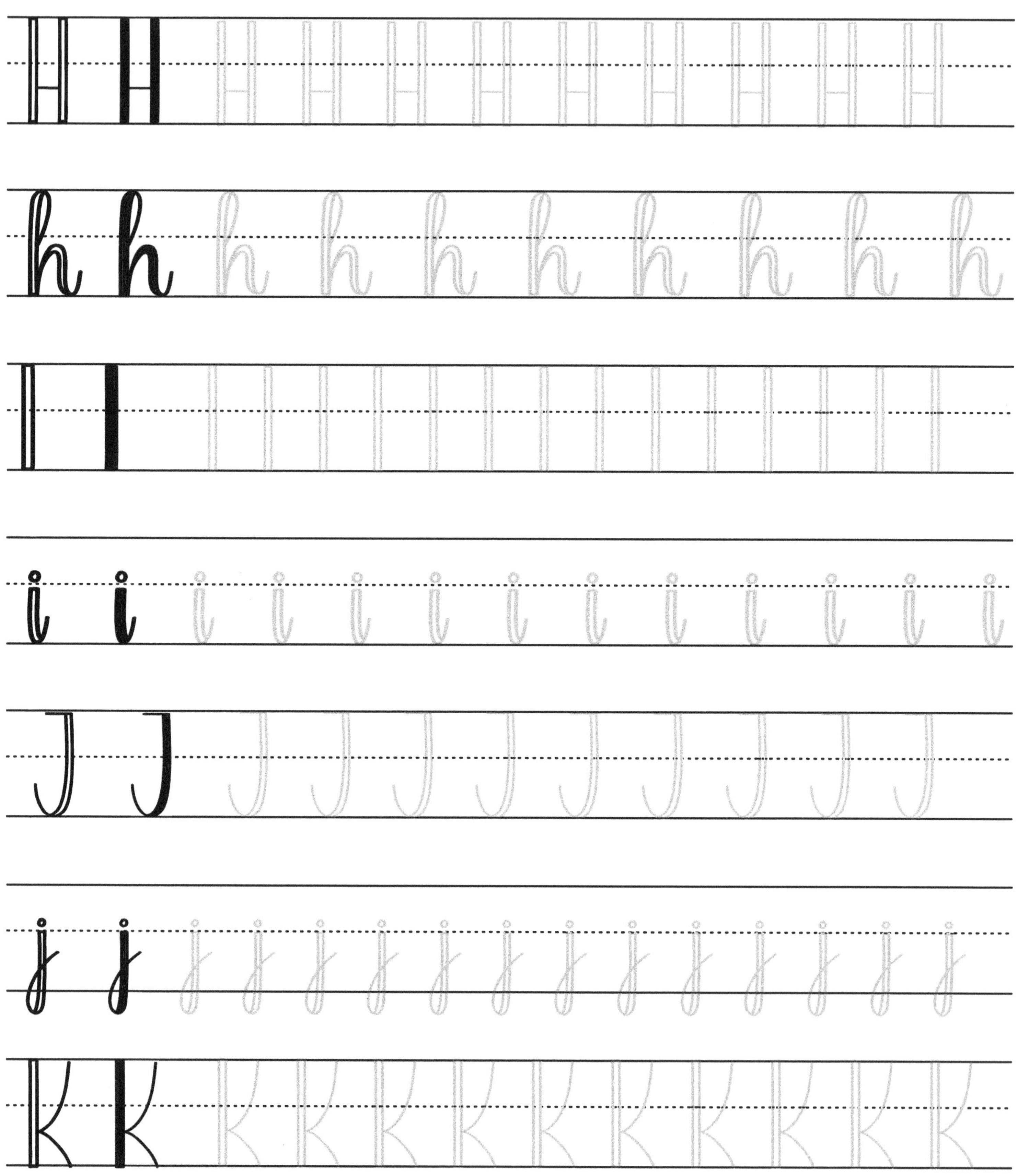

Practice Sheet

Basic Calligraphy

UPPERCASE AND LOWERCASE PRACTICE

Practice Sheet

Basic Calligraphy

UPPERCASE AND LOWERCASE PRACTICE

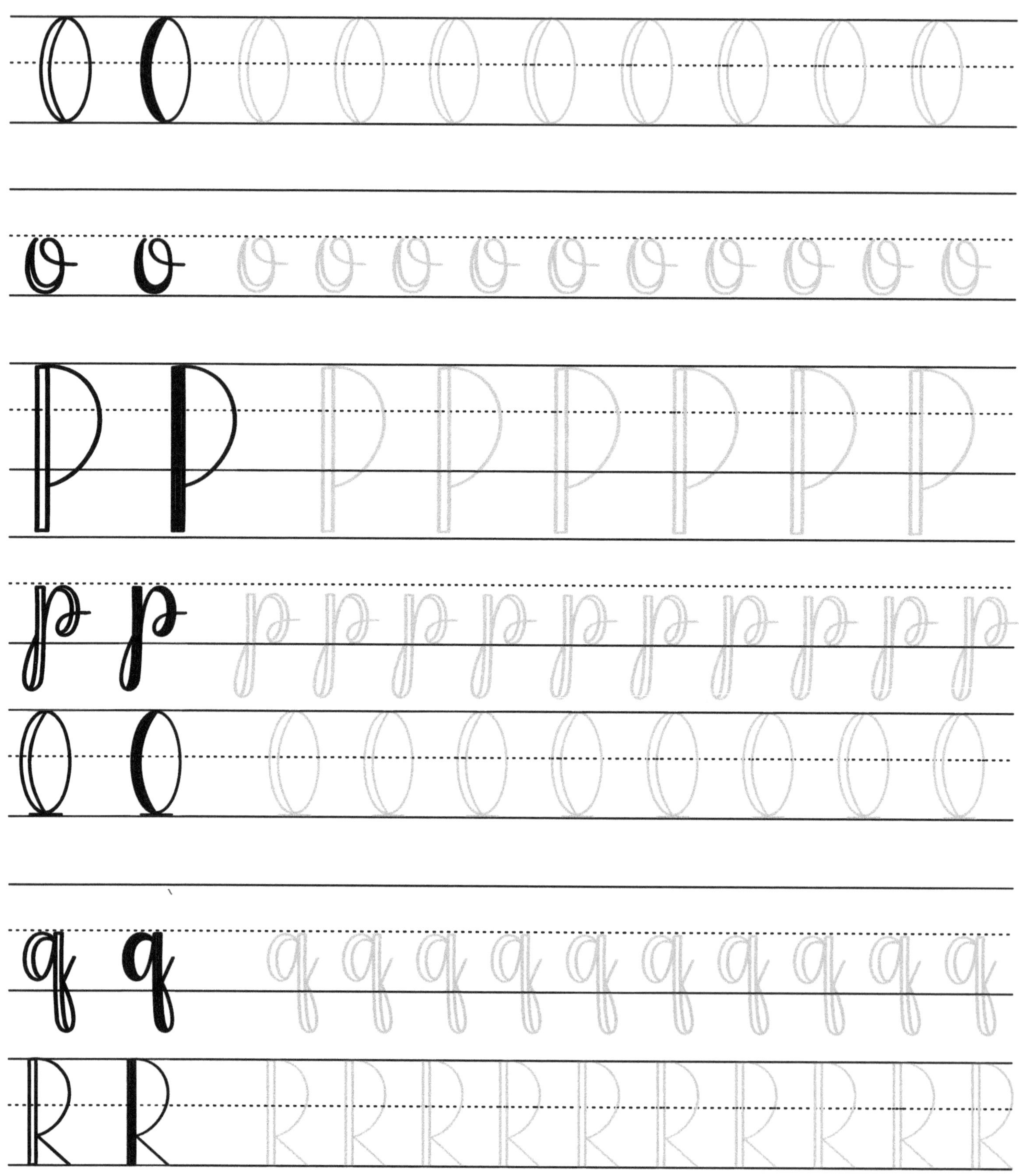

Practice Sheet

Basic Calligraphy

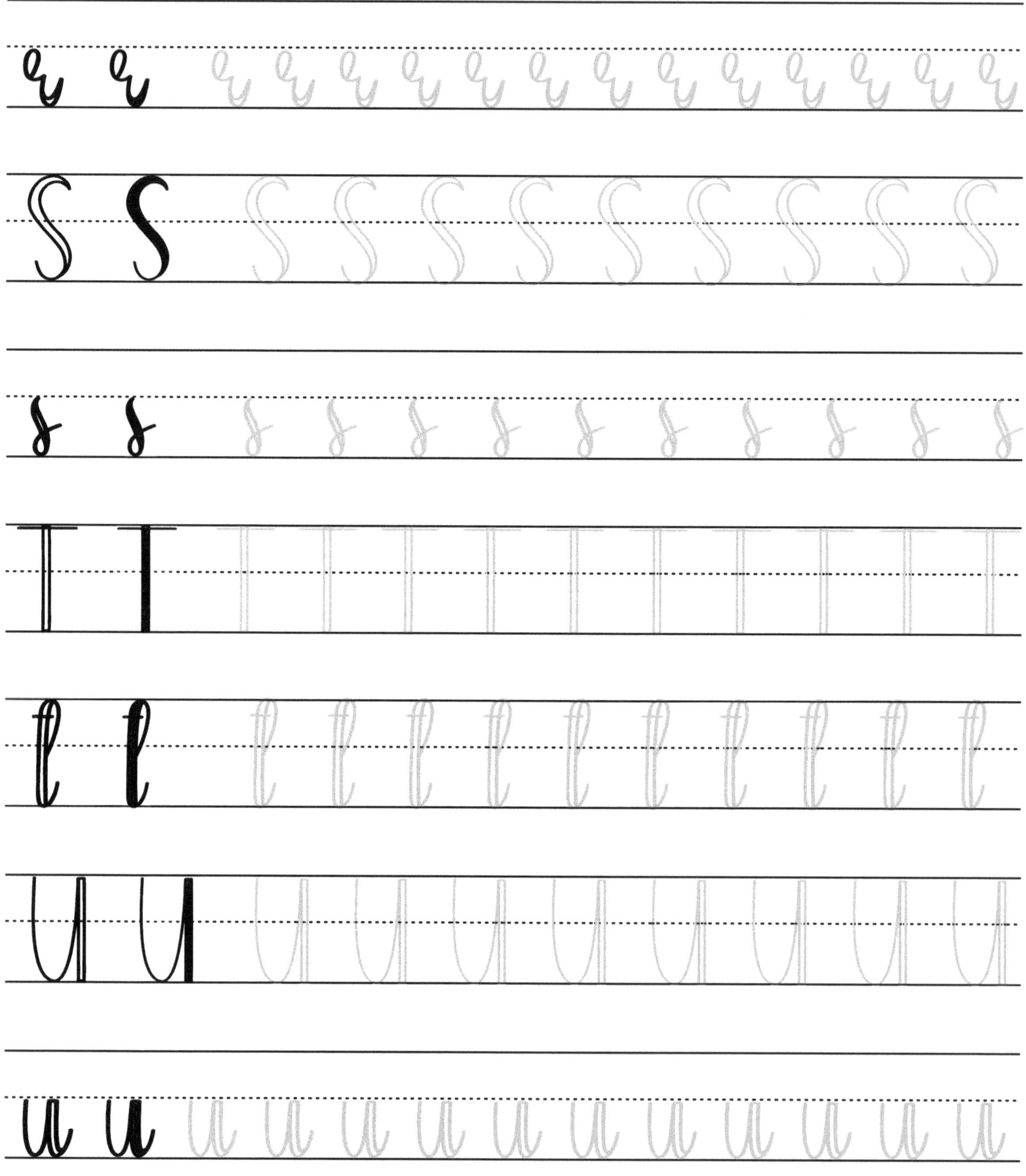

Practice Sheet

Basic Calligraphy

UPPERCASE AND LOWERCASE PRACTICE

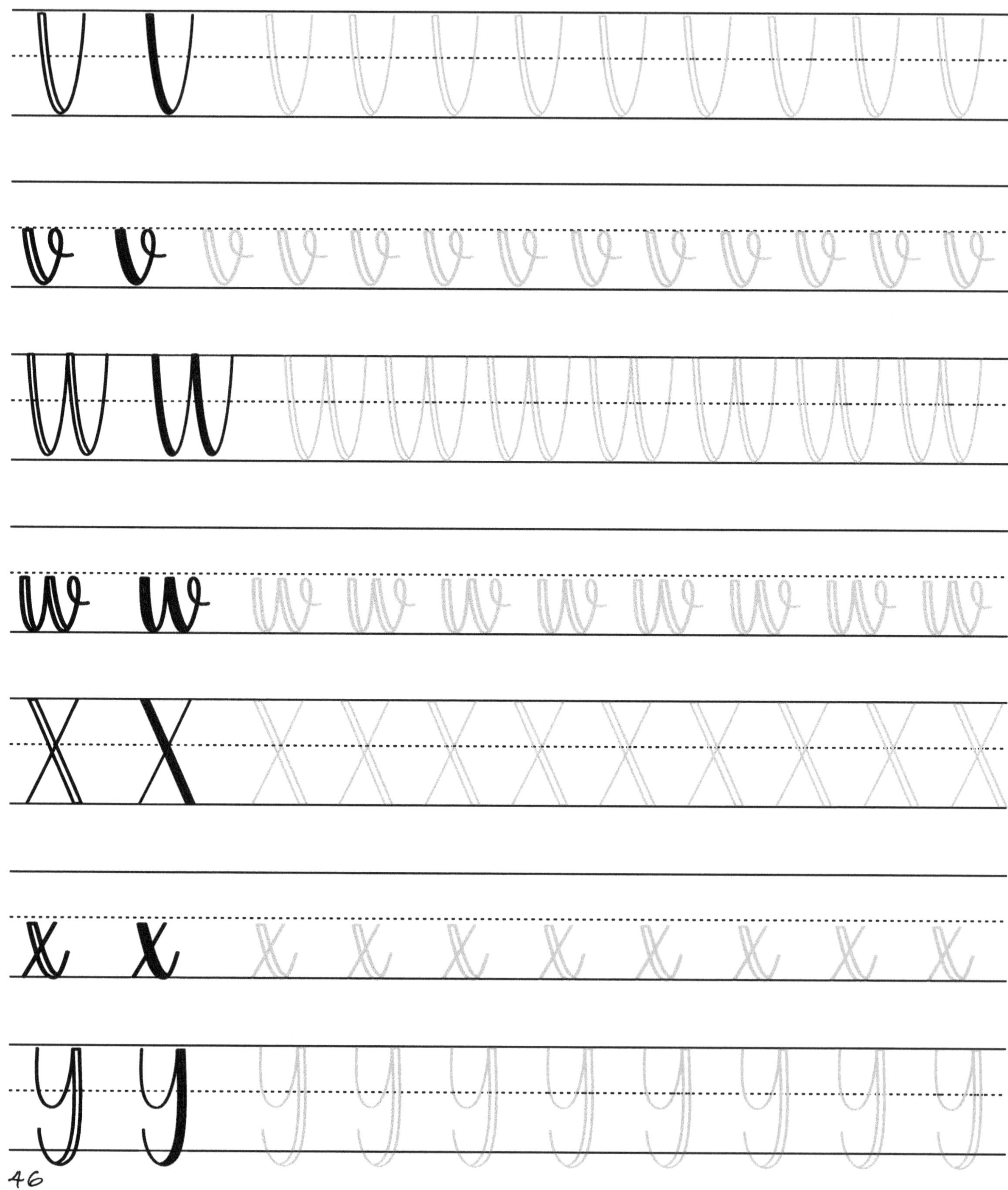

Practice Sheet

Basic Calligraphy

UPPERCASE AND LOWERCASE PRACTICE

Practice Sheet

Basic Calligraphy

NUMERIC DIGITS

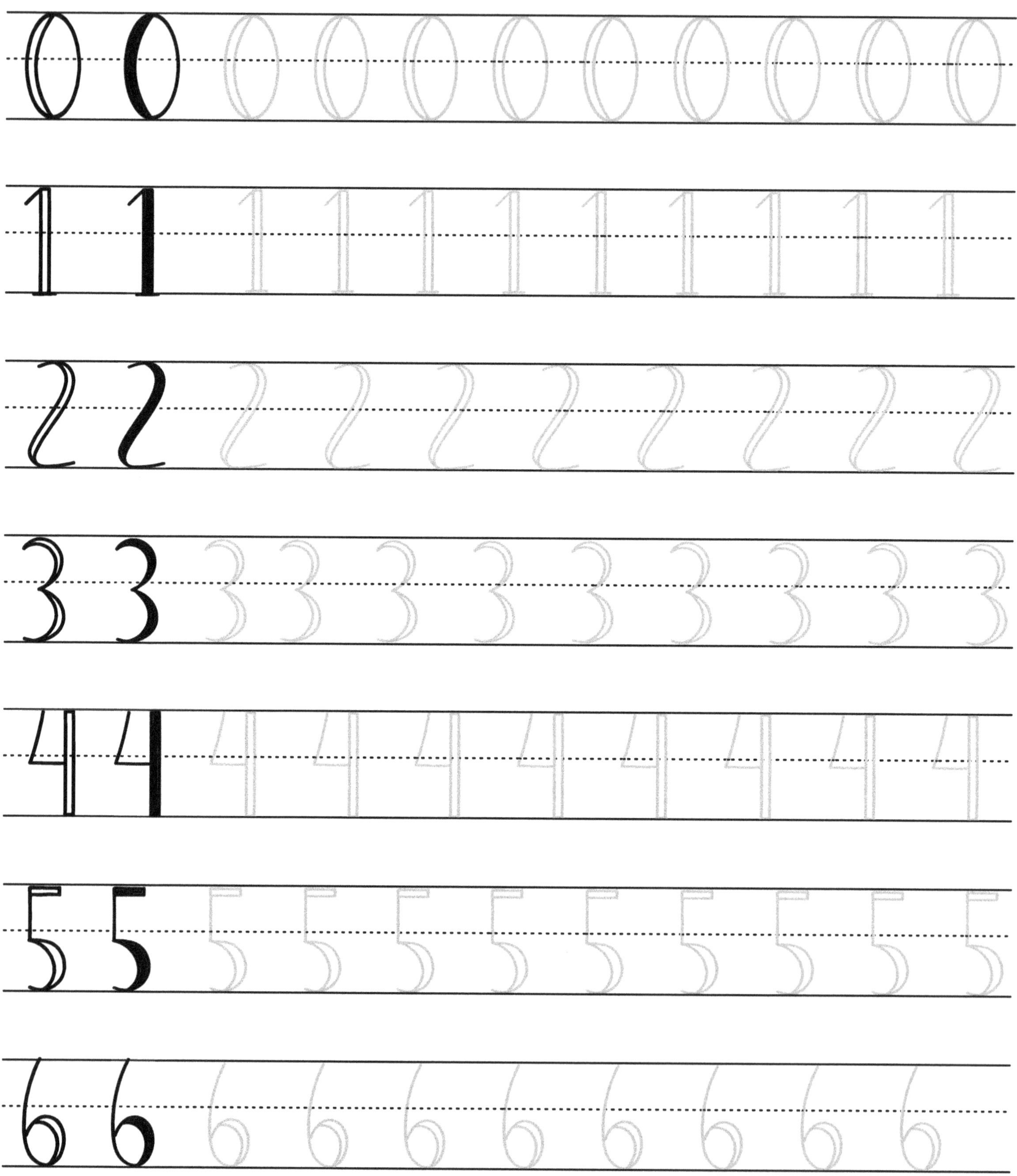

Practice Sheet

Basic Calligraphy

NUMERIC DIGITS

Practice Sheet

Basic Calligraphy

Writing

Love

Beauty

Thank you

Sweet

Hello

Life

Practice Sheet

Basic Calligraphy

WORD COMPLETION EXERCISE

Sun

Moon

Sea

Wine

Family

Happiness

Freedom

Practice Sheet

Basic Calligraphy

WORD COMPLETION EXERCISE

Dreams

Passion

Art

Flowers

Time

Music

Heart

Practice Sheet

Basic Calligraphy

WORD COMPLETION EXERCISE

Angel

Stars

Color

Perfume

Smile

Nature

Hope

Practice Sheet

Basic Calligraphy

WORD COMPLETION EXERCISE

Magic

Poetry

Pain

Air

Adventure

Beach

Mountain

Practice Sheet

Basic Calligraphy

PHRASES COMPLETION EXERCISE

Ink flows beautifully

Write with grace

Master every curve

Art through letters

Paper meets ink

Draw your words

Flourish your style

Practice Sheet

Basic Calligraphy

Letters come alive

Perfect every line

Ink your soul

Script with passion

Elegance in motion

Write your art

Feel every stroke

Practice Sheet

Basic Calligraphy

Flow with creativity

Ink shapes imagination

Lines build dreams

Letters hold stories

Capture every curve

Dance with ink

Shapes of beauty

Practice Sheet

Basic Calligraphy

Write your world

Embrace every letter

Lines create magic

Grace in script

Ink your vision

Words as art

Create timeless art

Practice Sheet

Basic Calligraphy

CREATIVE LETTERING INSPIRATION

Dream big, work hard

Create. Inspire. Repeat

Ink your story.

Make it beautiful

Every stroke matters.

Words shape worlds

Art is timeless.

Practice Sheet

Basic Calligraphy

July 20, 1969

First Moon Landing

December 25, 2025

Christmas Day

April 15, 1912

Titanic Sinks

Practice Sheet

Basic Calligraphy

November 9, 1989

Fall of the Berlin Wall

July 4, 1776

Independence Day

October 31, 2023

Halloween Night

The end

Practice Sheet

Practice Sheet

"I would like to express my gratitude for purchasing this book. I would be immensely thankful if you could take a moment to share your feedback. This greatly helps the growth of our small business and allows us to reach more people.."